How Do Graphics Cards Work?

Exploring GPU Architecture

The Unseen Force Powering Video Games,

Bitcoin Mining, and AI Breakthroughs

Joe E. Grayson

Table of Contents

Introduction

What if I told you that behind the dazzling worlds of video games, the uncanny intelligence of machines, and the ceaseless hum of cryptocurrency mining lies a single, unsung hero? It's not a miraculous innovation in software, nor is it some futuristic contraption straight out of a science fiction movie. It's something that many take for granted, often nestled discreetly inside a computer case: the graphics card. What enables a virtual warrior's armor to shimmer under digital sunlight? What lets a neural network analyze mountains of data and make life-changing predictions? What makes it possible to mint cryptocurrency at unfathomable speeds? The answer is the same—a silent workhorse called the GPU.

For decades, graphics cards were seen as tools for gamers, devices solely responsible for rendering polygons and textures to bring life to video games. But today, they are so much more than that. They power some of humanity's most profound technological advancements, silently bridging the gap between fantasy and reality. Every breathtakingly immersive video game, every self-learning artificial intelligence, every blockchain transaction is proof of their unparalleled might. The modern GPU is not just a piece of hardware; it is a cornerstone of our digital revolution.

In a world where computational power defines innovation, GPUs have quietly claimed their throne as the backbone of progress. From powering the awe-inspiring graphics of cinematic gaming experiences to training neural networks that predict the future of medicine,

GPUs operate on a scale that is almost incomprehensible. They perform trillions of calculations every second, transforming raw data into the lifelike visuals and groundbreaking discoveries that define our era. But how do they do it? How does this ingenious technology work? And why is it reshaping industries far beyond gaming?

This book is a journey into the heart of the GPU, a quest to uncover the hidden genius behind its architecture and the revolutionary impact it has on the world. Together, we'll strip away the technical jargon and explore the marvels of its design, its unparalleled computational power, and the reasons it outpaces traditional processors in tackling the most demanding tasks. Along the way, we'll uncover the story of how these silicon giants have evolved, their challenges, their triumphs, and their promise for the future.

Prepare yourself for an adventure into the unseen force driving our digital age. This is not just a story about technology; it's a story about how an innovation once considered niche is now shaping the future of humanity. By the end of this book, you'll not only understand the magic behind graphics cards but also appreciate their indispensable role in building the digital landscapes of tomorrow. Buckle up—this is the story of the GPU, and it's about to begin.

Chapter 1: The Power of Graphics Cards

In the mid-90s, a revolution quietly reshaped the gaming world. It was 1996 when *Super Mario 64* arrived, taking players from the flat, two-dimensional worlds of its predecessors into a fully realized 3D universe. For the first time, gamers could guide Mario in every direction, leap across platforms that felt tangible, and explore environments that hinted at depth and space. This was the dawn of 3D gaming—a moment that redefined the boundaries of what games could achieve. At the time, the visuals were groundbreaking, even magical, as the emerging technology brought pixels to life in ways no one had seen before.

Fast-forward to the present day, and the leap in graphical complexity is astonishing. Take a game like *Cyberpunk 2077*, where the streets of Night City burst with photorealistic detail. Neon lights reflect on rain-slick pavements, shadows adjust dynamically to shifting light sources, and characters display an eerie lifelike quality. Every surface, texture, and reflection feels as though it belongs in the real world rather than a virtual one. It's no longer just a game—it's an immersive experience, one where the line between reality and simulation blurs.

This evolution, from Mario's blocky adventures to the sprawling dystopian metropolis of *Cyberpunk 2077*, encapsulates the story of graphics technology's relentless march forward. What once required a few hundred million calculations per second to produce the simplistic landscapes of the 90s now demands trillions of calculations per second to render today's complex, dynamic worlds. This transformation is not merely about aesthetics; it's about the power to create universes from lines of code, each pixel and polygon a testament to the capabilities of modern GPUs.

The journey from simple 2D sprites to hyper-realistic 3D environments is a chronicle of human ingenuity. It's a reminder that every shimmering skyline and every intricately detailed character is a product of decades of innovation, where each generation of technology has pushed the boundaries of what we believed was possible. Graphics cards, those silent workers within our computers, have been at the heart of this revolution, enabling the incredible transition from pixels to immersive, living worlds.

In the early days of gaming, the computational requirements to bring a virtual world to life were modest by today's standards. A game like *Super*

Mario 64—a pioneering leap into 3D gaming—needed around 100 million calculations per second. At the time, this felt like an astonishing feat, a peak of technological achievement that made Mario's newfound freedom of movement feel revolutionary. But what once seemed like the pinnacle of computing power has now become a mere footnote in history. Today's games demand levels of computation that would have been unimaginable just a few decades ago.

Consider *Cyberpunk* 2077, a game that represents the cutting edge of modern graphics. To create its sprawling, hyper-realistic cityscapes, where every ray of light bounces, reflects, and diffuses just as it would in the real world, the computational demand skyrockets to a jaw-dropping 36 trillion calculations per second. This leap—from millions to trillions—isn't just a matter of scale; it's a transformation in what games can achieve, from simple geometric models to fully immersive digital realities that mimic the natural world with uncanny precision.

This immense computational power isn't just fueling gaming; it's reshaping industries far beyond entertainment. GPUs have become indispensable in fields that demand raw computational might and the ability to process vast amounts of data simultaneously. In artificial intelligence, GPUs power neural networks that can learn, predict, and make decisions, enabling breakthroughs in areas like medicine, autonomous vehicles, and natural language processing. They provide the parallel processing required to train AI models, crunching through data in days rather than months.

In the world of cryptocurrency, GPUs have played a pivotal role in Bitcoin mining. They once dominated the process, running the SHA-256 hashing algorithm millions of times per second to solve complex cryptographic puzzles and maintain the blockchain. Though now largely replaced by specialized ASIC machines, GPUs were instrumental in the early days of cryptocurrency, showcasing their versatility and ability to adapt to new computational challenges.

From gaming to AI to the financial frontier of cryptocurrency, GPUs have proven themselves as the ultimate workhorses of modern technology. They handle tasks at a scale and speed that CPUs could never hope to match, excelling in parallel processing where thousands of calculations must be performed simultaneously. As technology continues to evolve, it's clear that GPUs will remain at the heart of our digital transformation, driving progress in ways we're only beginning to understand.

Chapter 2: GPU vs. CPU – Understanding the Difference

The GPU and CPU, though often found working together inside a computer, are fundamentally different in their design and purpose, much like a team of specialists and a versatile jack-of-all-trades. The CPU, or Central Processing Unit, is the generalist. It is built to handle a wide variety of tasks, from managing the operating system to running applications, processing user inputs, and handling countless instructions that make a computer function smoothly. Its strength lies in flexibility, with a small number of cores optimized for speed and capable of processing complex, sequential tasks quickly and efficiently.

In contrast, the GPU, or Graphics Processing Unit, is a specialist in parallel data processing. Its architecture is designed to tackle massive volumes of similar calculations simultaneously, making it perfect for tasks like rendering images, transforming 3D models, or performing matrix computations. Where the CPU might excel at executing a single intricate task, the GPU thrives in scenarios requiring thousands or even millions of smaller calculations performed in parallel. Think of it as the difference between a sprinter and a relay team. The sprinter—a CPU—focuses on delivering a burst of speed for a short, focused task. The relay team—a GPU—divides the workload, ensuring all calculations are completed at once, albeit at a different pace.

This specialization in parallel processing is what makes GPUs indispensable for tasks like rendering video game graphics, training AI models, and mining cryptocurrencies. It's not that a CPU couldn't perform these tasks—it's that it would take significantly longer and consume far more power to do so. The GPU, with its thousands of cores working in unison, brings efficiency and speed to processes that demand it most.

Together, these two components form a symbiotic relationship. The CPU provides the flexibility and intelligence needed to oversee and coordinate tasks, while the GPU supplies the raw power to tackle the heavy computational lifting. It's this balance of general-purpose versatility and specialized efficiency that drives the capabilities of modern computers, enabling them to handle everything from the mundane to the extraordinary.

Imagine a bustling global economy where goods need to be transported efficiently. In this scenario, think of GPUs as massive cargo ships and CPUs as jumbo jets. Both are essential, but they serve very different purposes. A jumbo jet—the CPU—is built for speed and versatility. It can quickly carry passengers, urgent packages, or specialized cargo to a wide variety of destinations. It's agile, adaptable, and ideal for situations where time is of the essence. In contrast, the cargo ship—the GPU—is a titan of capacity. It moves immense volumes of goods across oceans, but at a slower, deliberate pace. Its strength lies in its ability to handle bulk, processing huge amounts of cargo with efficiency and scale.

This analogy captures the core differences between CPUs and GPUs. CPUs excel in speed and flexibility. With a smaller number of powerful cores, they are designed to perform a diverse range of tasks in rapid succession. From running operating systems to managing input devices, CPUs are the masterminds that keep a computer running smoothly. They shine when tackling sequential tasks that require a high degree of precision and responsiveness.

GPUs, on the other hand, trade speed for volume. With thousands of smaller, specialized cores, they are engineered to handle repetitive tasks across vast datasets. Whether rendering millions of pixels to create realistic images or processing parallel calculations for AI training, GPUs operate at a scale and efficiency that CPUs cannot match. They are purpose-built for scenarios where processing large amounts of similar data simultaneously is the priority.

The trade-off between speed and volume highlights why GPUs and CPUs are not competitors but collaborators. The CPU's flexibility allows it to manage diverse and complex operations, while the GPU's sheer power handles the heavy lifting in specific domains. Together, they create a balanced ecosystem, enabling modern computers to perform a wide array of tasks, from everyday computing to cutting-edge innovations.

This balance of speed and volume, flexibility and specialization, is what drives the remarkable capabilities of modern technology. Whether it's a jumbo jet racing across the skies or a cargo ship carrying the weight of the world, both are indispensable, working together to keep our digital and physical worlds moving forward.

Chapter 3: Inside a Graphics Card

Inside a graphics card lies a masterpiece of engineering, the GPU chip itself, often referred to as the heart of the system. Take, for example, the GA102 chip, a marvel of precision and scale. This single silicon die, packed with billions of transistors, is where the magic of parallel processing begins. Its surface is meticulously organized into clusters of processing cores, each one designed to execute trillions of calculations with breathtaking speed. It's here that the intricate dance of data unfolds, as instructions are issued, computations are performed, and results flow seamlessly.

But the GPU chip is only one part of a larger system. Surrounding it is a carefully designed ecosystem of components, all working in unison to ensure peak performance. Among these are the memory chips, the lifeblood of the GPU, which provide the high-speed data storage and retrieval needed to keep the cores fed with information. Modern graphics cards often use advanced memory like GDDR6X or GDDR7, capable of transferring terabytes of data per second. These chips ensure that the GPU has immediate access to the resources it needs, whether rendering a virtual world or training a neural network.

The printed circuit board, or PCB, acts as the foundation of the graphics card. It is a labyrinth of pathways connecting every component, ensuring that data flows efficiently between the GPU, memory chips, and external interfaces. It also houses critical components like voltage regulators, which convert the incoming power supply into the precise levels required by the

GPU. Without this fine-tuned power delivery, the GPU's performance would falter, or worse, the entire system could overheat or fail.

Speaking of heat, the cooling system is another essential piece of the puzzle. As the GPU processes trillions of calculations every second, it generates immense amounts of heat that must be dissipated to prevent damage. This is where heat sinks, thermal paste, and fans come into play. Heat pipes channel the thermal energy away from the GPU chip to radiator fins, where fans expel it into the surrounding air. In high-performance GPUs, advanced cooling solutions like liquid cooling may even be employed to ensure optimal temperatures.

Finally, there are the power modules and connectors, the unsung heroes that deliver the hundreds of watts required to keep the GPU running. Modern graphics cards often feature robust power connectors to draw energy directly from the power supply, ensuring the GPU has the juice it needs to handle the most demanding tasks.

Together, these components form a harmonious system, each piece indispensable to the card's overall function. The GPU may be the star of the show, but it relies on a finely tuned supporting cast to achieve its extraordinary feats. It's this intricate interplay of technology that allows a graphics card to not only meet the demands of modern computing but also push the boundaries of what's possible.

At the heart of a GPU lies a brilliantly organized structure, a hierarchy designed to harness its incredible computational power with precision and efficiency. This architecture, intricate yet purposeful, begins with the division of the GPU chip into clusters known as Graphics Processing Clusters (GPCs). Each GPC acts as a command center, orchestrating the work of smaller, more specialized units within it, ensuring the workload is distributed seamlessly across the chip.

Within each GPC are streaming multiprocessors (SMs), the versatile engines of the GPU. These multiprocessors are designed to handle parallel computations at scale, making them ideal for tasks that require massive amounts of data to be processed simultaneously. Each SM is home to multiple CUDA cores, the simplest and most numerous computational units in the GPU. These cores are like an army of calculators, each performing basic arithmetic operations at lightning speed. While their tasks may seem elementary, the sheer volume of CUDA cores working together enables the GPU to tackle incredibly complex problems with unparalleled efficiency.

But CUDA cores are just the beginning. Modern GPUs are also equipped with tensor cores, specialized units built to handle the matrix multiplications and additions that form the backbone of artificial intelligence and deep learning. These tensor cores excel in speeding up neural network computations, enabling GPUs to process vast datasets and train AI models in a fraction of the time it would take traditional processors. They're a critical component in driving advancements in machine learning, making tasks like image recognition, natural language processing, and generative AI not only possible but remarkably efficient.

Another cutting-edge innovation in GPU architecture is the inclusion of ray tracing cores.

These are larger and fewer in number compared to CUDA and tensor cores, but their purpose is highly specialized. Ray tracing cores simulate the behavior of light in a 3D environment, calculating how rays of light interact with surfaces, bounce off reflective materials, and cast shadows. This technology brings a level of realism to graphics that was once the domain of pre-rendered animations, making real-time ray tracing a reality in modern video games and visual effects.

This hierarchical design, with its specialized units and deliberate organization, is what makes the GPU a powerhouse of computation. Each level of the hierarchy, from clusters to multiprocessors to individual cores, plays a crucial role in enabling the GPU to handle an immense variety of tasks with speed and precision. Whether it's rendering stunning visuals, training cutting-edge AI models, or performing high-speed computations, the architecture of the GPU is a testament to the brilliance of modern engineering.

The journey of a GPU begins in the highly controlled environment of a semiconductor fabrication facility, where silicon wafers are transformed into the sophisticated chips that power modern graphics cards. This process involves etching billions of tiny transistors onto each wafer with an astonishing level of precision. However, even with the most advanced manufacturing techniques, perfection is unattainable. Dust particles, microscopic impurities, or subtle variations during fabrication can lead to defects in some areas of the chip.

This is where the practice of "binning" comes into play, a process that ensures no effort goes to waste. After the chips are manufactured, each one is rigorously tested to assess its functionality and performance. Chips that emerge unscathed, with all transistors and cores operating perfectly, are designated for the highest-end graphics cards, like the NVIDIA 3090 Ti. These flawless chips represent the pinnacle of performance and are priced accordingly.

For chips that contain minor defects, engineers step in to salvage their potential. Because of the hierarchical and repetitive design of GPUs, a defect in one area often affects only a small portion of the chip, such as a single streaming multiprocessor. Instead of discarding these chips, the defective section is isolated and deactivated, leaving the remaining cores fully operational. These chips are then used in slightly lower-tier models like the 3090, 3080 Ti, or 3080, with fewer active cores. For instance, while the 3090 may feature over 10,000 CUDA cores, the 3080 might have several hundred fewer due to these deactivated sections.

This approach is a brilliant example of resourcefulness in semiconductor manufacturing. By adapting the output based on chip quality, companies can maximize yield and reduce waste, offering consumers a range of products that cater to different performance needs and price points. This is why GPUs with the same underlying chip design, such as the GA102, can serve as the foundation for multiple graphics card models, each with varying specifications and capabilities.

Binning also extends beyond the number of active cores. The process involves testing clock speeds, power efficiency, and thermal performance, ensuring that each chip meets the specific requirements for the product it will become. A 3080, for instance, may be capable of slightly higher clock speeds than a 3070 because it passed more stringent performance tests during the binning process.

This meticulous categorization allows manufacturers to offer a diverse lineup of GPUs, each tailored to a specific segment of the market, while maintaining a high level of quality and reliability. It's a testament to the ingenuity of the manufacturing process, ensuring that even chips with imperfections can find their place in powering the digital world.

Chapter 4: How GPUs Handle Data

Parallel processing is the secret sauce that makes GPUs incredibly efficient at handling massive computational workloads. At its core, it's the idea of breaking down a problem into smaller, independent tasks and processing them simultaneously instead of one at a time. To achieve this, GPUs rely on specialized architectures that allow them to handle thousands, even millions, of calculations in parallel. Two foundational concepts underpinning this approach are SIMD, or Single Instruction Multiple Data, and SIMT, or Single Instruction Multiple Threads.

SIMD is a classic strategy in parallel computing, designed to execute a single instruction across multiple pieces of data simultaneously. Imagine a group of workers assembling identical parts of a machine—each worker follows the same set of instructions, but they each work on a different part. In the context of GPUs, SIMD allows a single instruction to be issued to a group of processing cores, each core performing the same operation on its respective chunk of data. This makes SIMD ideal for tasks like rendering graphics, where many calculations—like determining the color of a pixel or the position of a vertex—are independent but follow the same steps.

However, as computing needs evolved, so too did the demands on GPUs. Enter SIMT, a more advanced form of parallel processing. SIMT builds on the principles of SIMD but introduces greater flexibility. Instead of requiring every processing unit to stay locked in step with the same instruction, SIMT allows each thread to operate semi-independently. Think of it as a coordinated group of workers who can diverge slightly to handle specific tasks but still contribute to the overall goal. In GPU terms, this means that while a single instruction is still sent to a group of threads, individual threads can take slightly different paths depending on the data they're working with.

This flexibility is especially important in modern computing tasks, where not all data can be processed uniformly. For instance, when rendering a complex 3D scene, different sections of the image may require unique computations based on lighting, textures, or transparency. SIMT allows GPUs to manage these variations without sacrificing efficiency, ensuring that threads can branch when needed and reconverge when their paths align.

The evolution from SIMD to SIMT has been a game-changer for GPUs, enabling them to tackle a broader range of applications. Whether it's rendering lifelike graphics, training deep learning models, or performing scientific simulations, these architectures make it possible to process vast amounts of data with remarkable speed and efficiency. It's this ability to harness parallelism that sets GPUs apart, transforming them from graphics accelerators into the computational powerhouses driving innovation across industries.

Imagine a virtual world brimming with 3D objects—a cowboy hat on a table, a chair beside it, and a lamp casting light over the scene. Each of these objects starts as a collection of vertices in its own local coordinate system, often called *model space*. To bring these objects together into a unified scene, the GPU must transform these individual coordinates into a shared reference frame known as *world space*. This transformation is a critical step in rendering, setting the stage for everything that follows.

The process begins with the object's vertices, which are essentially points in 3D space defined by their X, Y, and Z coordinates. For example, the cowboy hat may have thousands of vertices that collectively define its shape. In its model space, the origin (0,0,0) might be at the center of the hat, and all the vertex coordinates are relative to that point. However, the hat doesn't exist in isolation—it needs to be positioned in the larger scene, relative to other objects like the table or the chair.

The GPU performs this transformation by applying a *translation matrix*, a mathematical operation that shifts the object from its model space to the appropriate location in world space. For each vertex, the GPU takes its original X, Y, and Z values and adds the position of the object in the world. For instance, if the hat's origin is at (5, 2, 3) in world space, every vertex in the hat's model space is shifted by that amount to align with its new position in the scene.

Next, the GPU might apply additional transformations, such as rotation or scaling. Rotation adjusts the orientation of the object, so the hat might tilt slightly to sit naturally on the table. Scaling changes the size of the object, ensuring the hat appears proportional to its surroundings. Each of these transformations is achieved through matrix operations, applied systematically to all the vertices of the object.

This process isn't limited to the cowboy hat; it's repeated for every object in the scene. The table, the chair, the lamp—all are individually transformed into world space using their own sets of matrices. By the end of this step, all the vertices exist in a common coordinate system, allowing the GPU to understand their spatial relationships.

The transformed vertices are then used to construct the triangles that define the surfaces of each object. These triangles are the building blocks of 3D rendering, providing the framework for textures, lighting, and shading. Once all the objects are placed in world space, the GPU continues its pipeline, determining which triangles are visible, how light interacts with them, and ultimately, how they appear on the screen.

Vertex transformation is just one step in the intricate dance of rendering, but it highlights the

GPU's ability to perform millions of calculations simultaneously. Each vertex transformation is independent of the others, making it an ideal task for the GPU's parallel processing capabilities. With thousands of cores working together, the GPU can transform entire scenes in real time, bringing virtual worlds to life with astonishing detail and realism.

Graphics memory is the lifeblood of a GPU, enabling it to process the vast amounts of data required for rendering stunning visuals or training sophisticated AI models. When a video game loads or a neural network begins training, terabytes of data—textures, vertex coordinates, lighting parameters, and more—must flow rapidly between the GPU and its memory. This is where advanced graphics memory technologies like GDDR6X and GDDR7 come into play, designed to keep up with the insatiable demands of modern computing.

GDDR memory, short for Graphics Double Data Rate, is built for speed and bandwidth, enabling GPUs to transfer enormous volumes of data in real time. GDDR6X, for instance, can achieve transfer rates of up to 1 terabyte per second. This bandwidth is critical for tasks like rendering high-resolution scenes, where the GPU needs immediate access to textures, models, and other assets to ensure a seamless experience. Imagine a bustling city in a video game, with thousands of unique elements—each element must be accessed and processed instantly to maintain fluidity and immersion.

The next step in this evolution is GDDR7, which takes data transfer efficiency to an entirely new level. To achieve these blistering speeds, engineers have developed advanced encoding schemes that allow more data to be transmitted with fewer signal wires. While earlier generations of memory relied on binary encoding—transmitting ones and zeros—modern memory like GDDR6X introduced PAM-4 (Pulse Amplitude Modulation), which uses four distinct voltage levels to encode two bits of data per signal.

GDDR7, however, refines this approach with PAM-3, an encoding scheme that uses three voltage levels—negative, zero, and positive—to transmit data. By combining these three levels in an optimized pattern, PAM-3 can encode binary data into ternary digits with remarkable efficiency. This reduces the complexity of the encoding process, lowers power consumption, and improves the signal-to-noise ratio, making it ideal for the high-speed, high-bandwidth demands of next-generation GPUs.

For example, PAM-3 encoding enables GDDR7 to send more data across the same number of signal wires compared to previous methods, while maintaining better reliability at extreme speeds. This is crucial in scenarios where the GPU must process and render terabytes of information in real time, such as when generating lifelike graphics or handling computationally intensive AI workloads.

The role of memory in a GPU's performance cannot be overstated. Without high-speed, efficient data transfer, the GPU's thousands of cores would sit idle, waiting for the data they need to complete calculations. Advanced memory technologies like GDDR6X and GDDR7 ensure that the GPU remains data-hungry, capable of performing tens of trillions of calculations per second without skipping a beat. These innovations not only enhance the GPU's performance but also pave the way for future advancements in gaming, AI, and beyond.

Chapter 5: Revolutionary Applications of GPUs

When you boot up a modern video game, you're stepping into a world that feels alive—vivid landscapes, dynamic lighting, and characters so detailed they seem almost tangible. Achieving this level of realism is no small feat; it's the result of an intricate process known as the rendering pipeline. This pipeline is a step-by-step sequence where raw data—vertices, textures, and lighting parameters—is transformed into the fully rendered images that appear on your screen, often in mere milliseconds.

The process begins with geometry. Every object in the game world is built from countless triangles, connected by vertices that define their shape. The GPU starts by processing these vertices, transforming them from their local model space into world space, then further into camera space. This ensures that every object is placed correctly in relation to the game's virtual camera. Once positioned, the GPU determines which triangles are visible and which are obscured, discarding any unnecessary ones to optimize performance.

Next comes rasterization, where the visible triangles are converted into pixels, the tiny dots that make up the final image on your screen. At this stage, textures are applied to give objects their color, detail, and material properties. For instance, a stone wall might receive a rough, uneven texture, while a glass surface would get a smooth, reflective one. The GPU also calculates lighting effects, determining how light sources interact with the surfaces in the scene to create shadows, highlights, and color variations.

Traditionally, these steps relied on approximations to simulate the effects of light. But with advancements in GPU technology, techniques like ray tracing have revolutionized real-time graphics. Ray tracing mimics the physical behavior of light, tracing individual rays as they bounce, reflect, and refract through the scene. This allows for incredibly realistic effects, such as reflections on water, the subtle interplay of light through a glass window, or the soft shadows cast by a flickering candle.

The challenge of ray tracing lies in its computational intensity. Simulating billions of light rays in real time would overwhelm even the most advanced GPUs, which is why ray tracing cores have been introduced. These specialized units within the GPU are designed to handle the complex calculations required for ray tracing, delivering stunning visuals without sacrificing performance.

The result is a leap in immersion. Games now feature environments that react dynamically to light, characters that feel grounded in their surroundings, and details that enhance storytelling. Whether it's the shimmering glow of neon lights in a cyberpunk city or the gentle play of sunlight through forest leaves, advanced rendering techniques transform games into experiences that captivate and transport players.

Real-time rendering pipelines, paired with innovations like ray tracing, showcase the raw power and sophistication of modern GPUs. They don't just create visuals—they craft entire worlds, bringing artistry and engineering together in perfect harmony to redefine what's possible in interactive entertainment.

In the realm of artificial intelligence and neural networks, GPUs have emerged as indispensable tools, enabling advancements that once seemed the stuff of science fiction. At the heart of this transformation lies the tensor core, a specialized unit within modern GPUs, designed to handle the computational backbone of AI: matrix multiplication. This operation is fundamental in training and running neural networks, where vast arrays of numbers must be multiplied and added together repeatedly to simulate how a brain processes information.

Imagine a neural network analyzing an image. Each layer of the network processes the data, extracting features like edges, shapes, and textures. To perform these tasks, the network relies on multiplying massive matrices—grids of numbers that represent the input data and the network's learned parameters. This is where tensor cores excel. They are purpose-built to handle matrix multiplication and accumulation operations with unparalleled speed and efficiency, performing these tasks simultaneously across thousands of cores.

The power of tensor cores becomes even more apparent in the context of generative AI. These models, such as those used in image generation, language modeling, or music composition, require billions, sometimes trillions, of calculations to learn and generate content. Each step involves feeding the model a dataset, performing matrix operations to analyze patterns, and refining its parameters. Without the parallel processing capabilities of GPUs, training these models would take weeks, even months. Tensor cores accelerate this process dramatically, reducing training times to days or hours.

Beyond training, GPUs are equally vital in running AI models. Tasks like real-time image recognition, natural language processing, and voice synthesis demand significant computational resources. GPUs enable these applications to function seamlessly, processing inputs and generating outputs in fractions of a second. This capability powers everything from virtual assistants to autonomous vehicles, allowing them to analyze their surroundings and make decisions almost instantaneously.

Generative AI, in particular, showcases the transformative role of GPUs. These models can create realistic images from scratch, write coherent essays, and even compose music that rivals human creativity. Such feats would be impossible without the computational horsepower that GPUs provide. Tensor cores make it feasible to process the staggering amounts of data required, while the GPU's architecture ensures these computations are completed in parallel, maintaining efficiency even under heavy workloads.

The role of GPUs in AI extends beyond raw computation. They've democratized access to machine learning, enabling researchers, startups, and hobbyists to experiment with AI on a scale previously reserved for large tech companies. From driving innovations in healthcare and autonomous systems to revolutionizing creative industries, GPUs have become the silent architects of a new era, pushing the boundaries of what AI can achieve.

In the world of AI, GPUs are more than tools; they are enablers of imagination and discovery, providing the computational foundation for technologies that are reshaping our understanding of intelligence and creativity. Tensor cores, with their unmatched efficiency in matrix operations, stand at the forefront of this revolution, making the impossible possible one calculation at a time.

In the early days of Bitcoin mining, GPUs were the workhorses that powered the network. To understand why, it's important to grasp the computational challenge at the heart of mining: solving the cryptographic puzzle of SHA-256 hashing. Bitcoin's blockchain relies on miners to process transactions and secure the network, and this is done by repeatedly running the SHA-256 algorithm on a set of input data. The goal is to produce a hash—a unique, fixed-length string of characters—that meets specific criteria, typically starting with a certain number of leading zeroes.

This process involves trial and error. Miners adjust a variable called a "nonce" (a random number) in the input data and run the SHA-256 algorithm over and over until they find a hash that satisfies the difficulty target. Each attempt is a completely independent computation, making the task an ideal candidate for parallel processing. GPUs, with their thousands of cores designed for handling parallel operations, were well-suited for this repetitive, high-volume workload.

In the early 2010s, Bitcoin miners realized that GPUs could perform SHA-256 hashing orders of magnitude faster than traditional CPUs. A CPU, with its limited number of cores, could process a few million hashes per second. Meanwhile, a GPU, leveraging its parallel architecture, could handle hundreds of millions of hashes per second. This efficiency made GPUs the go-to hardware for miners, and for a time, they dominated the Bitcoin mining landscape.

However, as Bitcoin's popularity grew, so did the network's mining difficulty. The increased competition meant miners needed even more computational power to stay profitable. GPUs, while efficient, began to struggle under the escalating demands of the network. This led to the development of ASICs, or Application-Specific Integrated Circuits—hardware specifically designed to perform SHA-256 hashing.

ASICs revolutionized Bitcoin mining. Unlike GPUs, which are versatile and designed for a variety of computational tasks, ASICs are purpose-built for a single function: mining Bitcoin. Their specialized design allows them to perform SHA-256 hashing at speeds far beyond what even the most powerful GPUs could achieve. A single ASIC can handle trillions of hashes per second, equivalent to the output of thousands of GPUs working in unison. Moreover, ASICs are far more energy-efficient, consuming less power per hash, which is critical for minimizing costs in an energy-intensive industry.

As a result, ASICs quickly replaced GPUs as the standard for Bitcoin mining. Today, GPUs are no longer competitive in the Bitcoin mining space, having been outclassed in both speed and efficiency. However, their legacy remains, as they were instrumental in Bitcoin's early growth and the broader adoption of blockchain technology.

While GPUs have moved on to power other computationally intensive tasks like AI and gaming, their role in the early days of Bitcoin mining highlights their versatility and adaptability. They may no longer dominate the mining landscape, but their impact on the cryptocurrency revolution is undeniable, having paved the way for the specialized hardware that now sustains the blockchain.

Chapter 6: Innovations and Future Trends

High Bandwidth Memory, or HBM, is a cutting-edge technology that revolutionizes the way data is stored and accessed in high-performance computing systems. Unlike traditional memory modules, HBM is designed to provide immense bandwidth and ultra-low latency by stacking memory dies vertically and connecting them using Through-Silicon Vias (TSVs). This unique design allows HBM to deliver data at speeds that far surpass conventional DRAM, making it ideal for the computationally intensive demands of modern AI chips.

The latest iteration, HBM3E, represents the pinnacle of this technology. It builds on the advancements of earlier generations to provide even greater capacity, speed, and efficiency. A single HBM3E memory cube can contain up to 36 gigabytes of memory, with multiple cubes often integrated around an AI chip to provide vast amounts of high-speed data storage. These memory stacks work seamlessly with the GPU or AI processor, ensuring that the processing cores are constantly fed with the data they need to perform trillions of calculations every second.

HBM3E is particularly crucial in the world of artificial intelligence, where models have grown exponentially in size and complexity. Training a state-of-the-art AI model involves processing massive datasets and performing countless matrix operations, all of which require rapid access to memory. Traditional memory architectures often struggle to keep up, creating bottlenecks that slow down training and inference times. HBM3E eliminates these bottlenecks by providing unparalleled bandwidth, allowing AI chips to access terabytes of data in seconds.

This high bandwidth is not just about speed; it also enables new levels of efficiency. HBM3E uses less power per bit transferred compared to traditional memory technologies, making it a more sustainable choice for energy-intensive applications. This efficiency is critical in AI data centers, where reducing power consumption translates to lower operating costs and a smaller environmental footprint.

The integration of HBM3E around AI chips also enables compact and streamlined designs. By stacking memory vertically, HBM reduces the physical space required for memory modules, allowing more components to fit within a single system. This is particularly advantageous in advanced AI accelerators, where space and thermal management are critical considerations.

In practice, HBM3E supports some of the most demanding AI workloads, from training large language models to running real-time inference in applications like autonomous driving and advanced robotics. Its combination of speed, efficiency, and capacity ensures that AI chips can handle the ever-growing computational demands of the future.

As AI continues to push the boundaries of what's possible, HBM3E stands as a cornerstone of this progress. It's not just a technological innovation; it's a fundamental enabler of the breakthroughs that define our era, powering the intelligence that shapes industries, enhances lives, and drives the future of human creativity.

The evolution of GPU design has been a journey of relentless innovation, driven by the need to process ever-increasing amounts of data more efficiently. One of the most significant advancements in recent years has been the transition from SIMD, or Single Instruction Multiple Data, to SIMT, or Single Instruction Multiple Threads. This shift has transformed how GPUs handle parallel processing, introducing a level of flexibility that was previously unattainable.

SIMD, the traditional approach to GPU processing, operates by executing a single instruction across multiple pieces of data simultaneously. While highly efficient for uniform tasks, such as applying the same calculation to every pixel on a screen, SIMD has its limitations. It requires all threads to remain in lockstep, executing the same instructions at the same time. This rigidity can create inefficiencies when tasks require divergent operations, as the GPU must wait for all threads to synchronize before continuing.

SIMT, on the other hand, adds a layer of sophistication. While still issuing a single instruction to multiple threads, SIMT allows each thread to progress at its own pace, with its own program counter. This means that threads can diverge when necessary, handling conditional branching or varying workloads without stalling the entire group. Modern GPUs leverage this flexibility to manage complex tasks more effectively, whether it's rendering dynamic game environments or training AI models with variable data inputs.

This architectural improvement has unlocked new possibilities for GPUs, enabling them to excel in diverse applications. The flexibility of SIMT is especially critical in AI and machine learning, where data dependencies and branching conditions are common. It also enhances the efficiency of gaming, where real-time rendering demands rapid adaptation to changing scenes and lighting conditions.

As GPUs continue to evolve, their potential in gaming, AI, and data centers is boundless. In gaming, the future points toward even more realistic environments, driven by advancements in ray tracing and real-time physics simulations. GPUs will likely incorporate more specialized cores for handling these tasks, delivering unparalleled immersion for players. The rise of virtual and augmented reality will further push GPU technology, requiring devices that can render complex 3D environments with minimal latency.

In AI, GPUs will remain at the forefront of innovation. The development of more efficient tensor cores and the integration of high bandwidth memory will enable GPUs to handle even larger models and datasets. This will accelerate breakthroughs in generative AI, autonomous systems, and real-time language processing, bringing AI applications closer to human-level performance.

Data centers, the backbone of modern computing, will also benefit from continued GPU advancements. The need for energy-efficient, high-performance computing will drive the adoption of GPUs optimized for large-scale parallelism. Innovations like liquid cooling and advanced fabrication techniques will ensure GPUs can deliver maximum performance while minimizing energy consumption, supporting the growing demands of cloud computing and AI-as-a-service platforms.

Looking ahead, GPUs are poised to become even more integral to the technological landscape. Their ability to adapt and evolve ensures they will continue to power the most demanding applications, from breathtaking virtual worlds to the transformative intelligence that shapes industries. As the boundaries of what GPUs can achieve expand, they will remain at the heart of our digital future, driving progress in ways we can only begin to imagine.

Chapter 7: The Hidden Challenges of GPUs

Modern GPUs are marvels of engineering, capable of performing trillions of calculations per second, but this incredible power comes with a cost: energy consumption. High-performance GPUs require immense amounts of electricity to function, especially when pushed to their limits in demanding tasks like gaming, AI training, and cryptocurrency mining. A flagship GPU can draw hundreds of watts under load, generating substantial heat as a byproduct. This heat must be managed efficiently to ensure stability and longevity, which is why advanced cooling systems—ranging from large heat sinks and multiple fans to sophisticated liquid cooling solutions—are essential components of modern graphics cards. However, these cooling systems add complexity, weight, and cost, making energy efficiency a key area for future innovation.

The challenges don't end with power consumption. The manufacturing process for GPUs is a delicate and complex affair, where even minor imperfections can have significant consequences. As GPUs are fabricated on silicon wafers, billions of transistors must be etched with nanometer precision. Despite cutting-edge technology, defects are inevitable. A single dust particle or slight variation in the process can render parts of a chip inoperable. To mitigate waste, manufacturers employ a process called binning, where chips are tested and sorted based on their performance and the functionality of their cores. Chips with minor defects are repurposed for lower-tier models by deactivating the defective sections. While this ensures most chips find a use, it also means that perfect, high-performance chips—used in flagship models—are rarer, driving up their price and sometimes causing shortages.

Beyond manufacturing, the environmental impact of GPUs raises serious sustainability concerns. The energy required to run GPUs, particularly in large-scale applications like cryptocurrency mining, contributes significantly to global electricity consumption. Mining farms, packed with thousands of GPUs or ASICs, operate around the clock, often relying on non-renewable energy sources. This has sparked debates about the environmental cost of cryptocurrencies and the broader implications of GPU power consumption.

Another pressing issue is e-waste. The rapid pace of technological advancement means GPUs often have a relatively short lifecycle, as users upgrade to newer, more powerful models. Discarded GPUs contribute to the growing problem of electronic waste, which is challenging to recycle due to the complexity of materials used. Improper disposal can lead to hazardous substances leaching into the environment, compounding the ecological footprint of these devices.

Addressing these challenges requires a multi-faceted approach. Manufacturers are already exploring ways to make GPUs more energy-efficient, from improving chip architecture to adopting more sustainable materials. The shift toward renewable energy in data centers and mining operations could significantly reduce the environmental impact of GPU-powered activities. Additionally, initiatives to extend the lifespan of GPUs through better repairability, second-hand markets, and recycling programs can help combat e-waste.

As GPUs continue to push technological boundaries, balancing performance with sustainability will become increasingly important. The industry faces the challenge of meeting the growing demand for computational power while mitigating its environmental and social impact. With thoughtful innovation and responsibility, GPUs can drive progress without compromising the planet's future.

Conclusion

As we close this journey into the fascinating world of GPUs, it's clear that these powerful devices are far more than just hardware components. They are the engines driving modern technology, transforming raw data into breathtaking visuals, intelligent decisions, and groundbreaking innovations. From the intricate architecture of CUDA cores, tensor cores, and ray tracing units to the vast applications in gaming, AI, and cryptocurrency, GPUs have redefined the limits of what machines can achieve. Their evolution—from simple accelerators of 2D graphics to the computational giants powering our digital world—stands as a testament to human ingenuity.

GPUs are not just tools; they are the lifeblood of the digital revolution. They enable the immersive virtual worlds of gaming, bring AI models to life by crunching mountains of data, and even underpin the decentralized networks that shape the financial future. Their impact spans industries and disciplines, making them indispensable in solving the challenges of today and unlocking the possibilities of tomorrow.

Yet, beyond their technical brilliance lies an inspiring story of how innovation, resourcefulness, and relentless curiosity continue to push boundaries. Understanding the complexity behind a graphics card—the careful hierarchy of its design, the precision of its manufacturing, and the sheer scale of its computational power—reveals the extraordinary effort that goes into creating the technology we often take for granted.

This book is a celebration of that effort. As you fire up your favorite video game, interact with an AI assistant, or read about the latest advances in technology, pause for a moment to appreciate the hidden genius of the GPU. Behind the screens, trillions of calculations are performed every second, powered by a symphony of engineering marvels, each working in perfect harmony to shape your experience.

The story of GPUs is far from over. As their capabilities grow and their applications expand, they will continue to shape the world in ways we can only imagine. Whether you're a gamer, a technologist, or simply someone curious about the forces shaping our modern world, take a moment to marvel at the complexity, ingenuity, and potential of this technology.

The next time you see stunning graphics, hear about a breakthrough in AI, or learn of innovations in blockchain, know that behind it all lies the power of the GPU—a testament to the limitless possibilities of human innovation. Let's not just use this technology but cherish the brilliance that makes it all possible.